D1171766

Getting Started
•with•
Model Trains

A young boy is the engineer of this 0/027 Gauge RailScope™ locomotive. Using a miniature video camera mounted inside the locomotive, he can also view his layout as if he were standing inside the cab of the engine. The sense of actually "being there" on your model train layout is an experience not available before RailScope from Lionel Trains (also see front cover).

Back cover photo, courtesy of Gebr. Marklin & Cie, GmbH, Goppingen, W. Germany, shows a busy station with a multitude of miniature passengers.

Getting Started
·with·
Model Trains

John Townsley

Sterling Publishing Co., Inc.   New York

The Lionel Freight Flyer™ is pulled by a black steam locomotive with a working headlight. A slope-back coal tender, royal-blue boxcar, green gondola with removable cargo canisters and a bright red square-window caboose complete the set. (Track and a U.L. approved transformer are also included.)

Library of Congress Cataloging-in-Publication Data

Townsley, John.
    Getting started with model trains / John Townsley.
        p.   cm.
    Includes index.
    ISBN 0-8069-7362-5
    1. Railroads—Models.   I. Title.
    TF197.T585   1991
    625.1′9—dc20   90-24057
                                                           CIP

10 9 8 7 6 5 4 3 2 1

© 1991 by John Townsley
Published by Sterling Publishing Company, Inc.
387 Park Avenue South, New York, N.Y. 10016
Distributed in Canada by Sterling Publishing
c/o Canadian Manda Group, P.O. Box 920, Station U
Toronto, Ontario, Canada M8Z 5P9
Distributed in Great Britain and Europe by Cassell PLC
Villiers House, 41/47 Strand, London WC2N 5JE, England
Distributed in Australia by Capricorn Ltd.
P.O. Box 665, Lane Cove, NSW 2066
Manufactured in the United States of America
All rights reserved

Sterling ISBN 0-8069-7362-5

Contents

The Lionel Badlands Express™ train set is led by an 0-4-0 steam locomotive, followed by a horse carrier car with fences, operating cowboy car and a Southern Pacific payroll car. Two horses, a pair of desperadoes and two railroad guards are also included.

1

The Magic of Model Railroading

As your train roars down the track, blowing its whistle, signal lights change color and crossing gates lower. A gateman leaves his shanty and waves to the oncoming train. Meanwhile, at a nearby siding, a coal elevator unloads its cargo into a waiting gondola. On an adjacent track, cattle and horses walk through corrals and into stock cars. In model railroading, you are the "engineer" directing these exciting scenarios from your control panel.

Model trains are exciting. They move with speed in all directions and are more fascinating than most other toys, combining entertainment with history and business. Add to this a vast selection of miniature equipment and accessories, and you can have the hobby of a lifetime. Model railroading is a pastime for all ages. More than a quarter of a million Americans and many more overseas engage in this popular leisure-time activity.

The interest in model trains stems from our fascination with real railroads and the desire to capture them in miniature. Model trains have set a tradition that originated in the middle of the 19th century and has lasted more than 150 years.

Operating your trains can be a pleasant escape from the routines of daily life. At the press of a button, you can couple and uncouple your rolling stock, load and unload a variety of freight cars and activate many animated accessories. Modern control systems allow you to duplicate the throttle and brake action of real locomotives and route your trains through switches to various tracks on your layout.

Model railroading provides a chance for you to exercise your creative abilities. You can design towns and villages, mountains and valleys, roads and bridges—all connected by rail in your own miniature three-dimensional world. You may wish to control the movement of trains yourself or set up elaborate signal systems and completely automate your layout.

Gathering around your layout is a social event. It is a great time when

The Lionel Cannonball Express™ is pulled by a tough black steam locomotive outfitted with a working headlight and a matching oil tender with chugging sound effects. It pulls a gray Erie Lackawanna boxcar, a brown Reading hopper, a black and yellow flatcar, and a red square-window caboose. Road signs, telephone poles, and a snap-together extension bridge complete the set. (Track and a U.L. approved transformer are also included.)

you get together with your friends and "run the trains." You will feel a sense of accomplishment when they ask if you built the layout all by yourself.

Your model train layout will be ever-changing. As you think of new ideas and new products are made, you will incorporate these into your railroad empire. Model railroading is a continuing hobby that you will enjoy for years and years.

The Industrial Starter Set from LGB will make it easy to start your LGB railway. The set includes a locomotive, freight cars, a full circle of track, transformer and some people figures to make your layout come alive.

Sizes and Gauges

Model trains come in a variety of sizes. If you have space limitations, the smaller sizes, such as HO or N, may be best suited for you. HO gauge is $\frac{1}{87}$th the size of its real-life original and tiny N gauge is $\frac{1}{160}$th. Many trains can be operated on a small layout with these sizes. The larger O gauge, $\frac{1}{48}$ proportion, provides a dramatic effect when operated on a big layout. S gauge, at $\frac{1}{64}$ of life size, is between HO and O. TT gauge is $\frac{1}{120}$th and 1 gauge, the largest, is $\frac{1}{32}$nd. Tiny Z gauge, introduced by Marklin in the early 70s, is the smallest gauge available.

Gauge is actually the distance between rail heads on the track. HO gauge trains run on track with $\frac{5}{8}$ of an inch span between each rail. O gauge track has a distance of $1\frac{1}{4}$ inches and S gauge is $\frac{7}{8}$ of an inch.

The large 1 gauge has gained popularity in the past few years. Spawned by the German manufacturer, Lehmann-Gross-Bahn, other train makers

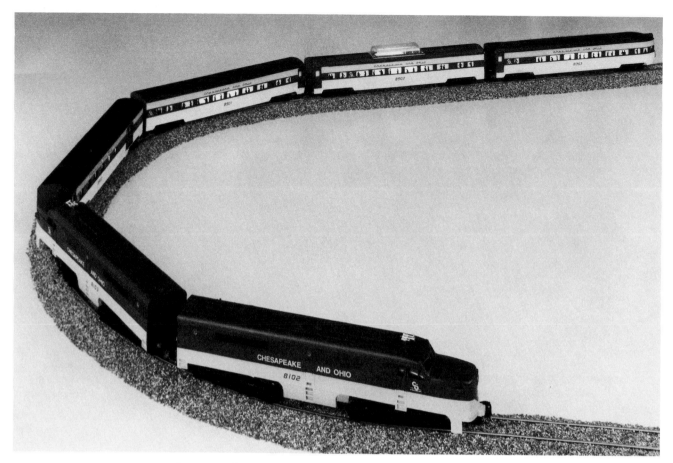

Serving urban centers from Chicago to Virginia is the Historic American Railroad #7 Chesapeake and Ohio passenger train. The American Flyer® C & O train in S gauge is powered by two PA-1 diesel locomotives in distinctive blue, yellow, and grey markings. Four illuminated passenger cars complete the set.

have scrambled to start producing trains of this size. LGB trains, called G gauge, are actually 1:22.5 scale and run on 1 gauge track.

Life-Like's quality workmanship is evident in this Bangor & Aroostook diesel. The model offers superior performance and is highly detailed.

Scale and Tinplate

Scale refers to the ratio in size between a model and its prototype. Scale equipment is measured to the exact scale size of its real railroad counterparts. Scale items often come in kit form. If you like to build and use your hands, then scale is right for you. Kits are available from the easy-to-assemble snap-together type to the more complex "craftsman" kits where a variety of hobby tools is needed. Some modelers engage in scratch-building. Using bits and pieces of wood and metal, plus a few manufactured parts like wheels and couplers, they create their own unique model railroad items. Scratch-building kits can be purchased at most hobby shops.

Tinplate is an old term dating back to the days when model trains were fabricated from tinplate stock. It is used today to describe ready-to-run trains, such as those made by Lionel Trains. Lionel has always been one of the most popular brands of toy trains in America.

Today, Lionel produces trains in O gauge and its new large scale, which corresponds to 1 gauge. The company's "Collector Series" includes replicas of locomotives, rolling stock and accessories that were produced years ago. The firm also makes American Flyer trains in S gauge.

Many companies throughout the United States manufacture model trains in various gauges and scales. Foreign trains from around the world are available at hobby shops. Names such as Athearn, Bowser, Fleischmann, Hornby, Kato, LGB, Marklin and Rivarossi are synonymous with quality model trains and accessories.

Puffing live steam, this large scale (1 inch = 1 foot) Republic locomotive was built by Carl Bellinger, famous World War I pilot. (Courtesy Charles Schaefer, Caboose, Inc.)

Live Steam

The sight and sounds of a miniature live-steam train winding its way along an outdoor track has attracted many hobbyists to get involved with this aspect of the hobby. A large backyard is most suitable for such a project. Real trees and bushes serve as scenery. Most "garden" railways are built in 1 gauge, although O gauge is sometimes used. Care should be taken to use weather-resistant track and accessories to help withstand the harshness of the elements.

Live-steam locomotives generally contain modern liquid fuel burners rather than ones fired by coal. Remote control devices are sometimes incorporated to start, stop and control the speed of the trains. A growing number of commercial kits and ready-to-run models are available for the live-steam devotee.

The doors of LGB cars can be opened. Figures can be placed on the train or the layout. Freight can be loaded and unloaded. Uncoupling tracks permit realistic switching. Plenty to do.

Model Railroading Costs

As with many hobbies, model railroading can be as inexpensive or costly as you elect to make it. Trains and accessories range in price from a few dollars to a few hundred dollars. You don't have to buy everything at once. After your basic layout is completed, you can add items as your budget allows.

Today's modern production methods have made model trains available at reasonable prices. Generally, smaller-gauge items cost less than their larger-gauge counterparts, but you'll have to buy more of them to fit in the space that the larger gauges use. O gauge track costs about one dollar and fifty cents per foot. HO and N gauges are half as much and G gauge is more than double the cost of O gauge.

A superb layout is not necessarily the product of a large investment of money; instead it may be the result of an investment in planning and design.

A corner drug store in HO gauge. Molded in five colors, this finely detailed building kit from Tyco will look good on any layout.

COST OF BUILDING A TABLETOP LAYOUT

Benchwork

4 × 8 Plywood Board	$25.00
Homosote Board	14.50
2 × 4s @ 30 cents per foot	28.50
Nails and Braces	7.00
Paint	15.00
TOTAL	90.00

Scenery

Artificial Grass (3 bags)	12.00
Track Ballast (3 bags)	6.00
Ballast Cement (3 cans)	12.00
Screen Material (36 sq. ft. @ 25 cents per sq. ft.)	9.00
Modeling Compound (3 boxes)	12.00
Artificial Trees	9.00
TOTAL	60.00

Estimated costs for a standard tabletop layout with an average amount of scenery. Prices may be higher or lower than those stated.

Constructing custom buildings for your train layout is made easy with these special wood shapes from Midwest Products Company. They are available in cherry and balsa.

MATERIALS FOR A 4 × 8 LAYOUT

Frame

2 pieces 2 × 4 — 8 ft. long
8 pieces 2 × 4 — 4 ft. long
Flathead screws — 2½ in.

Legs

8 pieces 2 × 4 — 34½ in. long
8 carriage bolts with nuts & washers

Lower Frame

2 pieces 2 × 4 — 8 ft. long
2 pieces 2 × 4 — 4 ft. long

Tabletop

1 piece 4 × 8 plywood — ¾ in. thick
1 piece 4 × 8 insulating board — ½ in. thick
Flathead screws — ⅝ in.

Santa can give his reindeer a rest and ride in warmth this coming holiday season with the Lionel Large Scale™ North Pole Railroad train set. Featured in this set is a green 0-4-0T steam engine with Santa at the controls, a white flatcar with packages and a red bobber caboose.

Model Train Manufacturers

O Gauge

Bachmann Industries Inc., 1400 E. Erie Avenue, Philadelphia, PA 19124
Bowser Manufacturing Co., 21 Howard Street, Montoursville, PA 17758
ISLE Laboratories, P.O. Box 636, Sylvania, OH 43560
Kadee Quality Products, 720 S. Grape Street, Medford, OR 97501
Life-Like Products, Inc., 1600 Union Avenue, Baltimore, MD 21211
Lionel Trains, Inc., 26750 23 Mile Road, Mount Clemens, MI 48045
MDK, Inc., P.O. Box 2831, Chapel Hill, NC 27515
Model Power, 180 Smith Street, Farmingdale, NY 11735
Right-of-Way Industries, P.O. Box 13036, Akron, OH 44313
Walthers, Inc., 5601 West Florist Avenue, Milwaukee, WI 53218

HO Gauge

Athearn, 19010 Laurel Park Road, Compton, CA 90222

Bachmann Industries, Inc., 1400 E. Erie Avenue, Philadelphia, PA 19124

Bowser Manufacturing Company, 21 Howard Street, Montoursville, PA 17754

ISLE Laboratories, P.O. Box 636, Sylvania, OH 43560

Intermarket, USA, 9060 NW 13th Terrace, Miami, FL 33172

Kadee Quality Products, 720 S. Grape Street, Medford, OR 97501

Kraemer Mercantile Corp., 200 5th Avenue, New York, NY 10010

Life-Like Products, Inc., 1600 Union Avenue, Baltimore, MD 21211

Mantua Industries, Inc., Grandview Avenue, Woodbury Heights, NJ 08097

Marklin, Inc., 16988 W. Victor Road, New Berlin, WI 53151

Model Die Casting, Inc., 3811 W. Rosecrans Boulevard, Hawthorne, CA 90250

Model Power, 180 Smith Street, Farmingdale, NY 11735

Model Power Mfg Co., Inc., 200 5th Avenue, New York, NY 10010

Overland Models, Inc., 5908 Kilgore Avenue, Muncie, IN 47304

Steven International, P.O. Box 126, Magnolia, NJ 08049

Super Scale Models, 200 5th Avenue, New York, NY 10010

Tyco Toys, Inc., 6000 Midlantic Drive, Mount Laurel, NJ 08054

Walthers, Inc., 5601 W. Florist Avenue, Milwaukee, WI 53218

Woodkrafter Kits, 42A N. Elm Street, Yarmouth, ME 04096

N Gauge

Atlas Tool Company, 378 Florence Avenue, Hillside, NJ 07205

ISLE Laboratories, P.O. Box 636, Sylvania, OH 32560

Kato USA, Inc., 781 Dillon Drive, Wood Dale, IL 60191

Kaydee Quality Products, 720 S. Grape Street, Medford, OR 97501

GAUGES OF MODEL TRAINS

Gauge	Scale Ratio	Track Gauge
1	32:1	1.75 inches
O	48:1	1.26 inches
S	64:1	0.875 inches
OO	76:1	0.648 inches
HO	87:1	0.648 inches
TT	120:1	0.471 inches
N	160:1	0.353 inches
Z	220:1	0.255 inches

Life-Like Products, Inc., 1600 Union Avenue, Baltimore, MD 21211
Model Die Casting, Inc., 3811 W. Rosecrans Boulevard, Hawthorne, CA 90250
Model Power, 180 Smith Street, Farmingdale, NY 11735
Model Power Mfg Co., 200 5th Avenue, New York, NY 10010
Steven International, P.O. Box 126, Magnolia, NJ 08049
Super Scale Models, 200 5th Avenue, New York, NY 10010
Walthers, Inc., 5601 W. Florist Avenue, Milwaukee, WI 53218

Z Gauge

ISLE Laboratories, P.O. Box 636, Sylvania, OH 43560
Kaydee Quality Products, 720 S. Grape Street, Medford, OR 97501
Marklin, Inc., 16988 W. Victor Road, New Berlin, WI 53151
Walthers, Inc., 5601 W. Florist Avenue, Milwaukee, WI 53218

S Gauge

American Models, 10088 Colonial Drive, South Lyon, MI 48178
Lionel Trains, Inc., 26750, 23 Mile Road, Mt. Clemens, MI 48045

1 Gauge

American Standard Car Co., P.O. Box 394, Crystal Lake, IL 60014
Aristo-Craft Distinctive Miniatures, 200 5th Avenue, New York, NY 10010
Galoob Toys, Inc., 500 Forbes Boulevard S., San Francisco, CA 94080
GHB International, P.O. Box 4063, Gaithersburg, MD 20885
ISLE Laboratories, P.O. Box 636, Sylvania, OH 43560
Kalamazoo Trains, 655 44th Street, Allegan, MI 490
LGB of America, Inc., 6444 Nancy Ridge Drive, San Diego, CA 92121
Life-Like Products, Inc., 1600 Union Avenue, Baltimore, MD 21211
Lionel Trains, Inc., 26750 23 Mile Road, Mount Clemens, MI 48045
Marklin, Inc., 16988 W. Victor Road, New Berlin, WI 53151
Model Die Casting, Inc., 3811 W. Rosecrans Boulevard, Hawthorne, CA 90250
Model Power, 180 Smith Street, Farmingdale, NY 11735
Model Power Mfg Co., 200 5th Avenue, New York, NY 10010
Railway Express Agency, 346 Bergen Avenue, Jersey City, NJ 07304
Walthers, Inc., 5601 W. Florist Avenue, Milwaukee, WI 53218

Model Train Accessories

ABACO International, P.O. Box 4082, Irvine, CA 92716
Aristo-Craft Distinctive Miniatures, 200 5th Avenue, New York NY 10010
B&B Models, P.O. Box 1067, Glen Ellyn, IL 60139
Bachmann Industries, Inc., 1400 E. Erie Avenue, Philadelphia, PA 19124
Brio Scanditoy Corp., 6555 Mill Road, Milwaukee, WI 53218
Bullyland Toys, Inc., 36 West 25th Street, New York, NY 10010
Cogin Industries, 200 5th Avenue, New York, NY 10010
Davis Grabowski, Inc., 6350 NE 4th Avenue, Miami, FL 33138
Dealer's Hobby Supplier Corp., 577 Scott Street, Memphis, TN 38112
Galoob Toys, Inc., 500 Forbes Boulevard S., San Francisco, CA 94080
GarGraves Trackage Corporation, RD 1, Box 255A, North Rose, NY 14516
ISLE Laboratories, P.O. Box 636, Sylvania, OH 43560
Kadee Quality Products, 720 S. Grape Street, Medford, OR 97501
Kalamazoo Toy Train Works, 541 Railroad Street, Bangor, MI 49013
Life-Like Products, Inc., 1600 Union Avenue, Baltimore, MD 21211
Lionel Trains, Inc., 26750 23 Mile Road, Mount Clemens, MI 48045
MDK, Inc., P.O. Box 2831, Chapel Hill, NC 27515
Marklin, Inc., 16988 W. Victor Road, New Berlin, WI 53151
Midwest Products Company, 400 S. Indiana Street, Hobart, IN 46342
Minicraft Models, Inc., 1510 W. 228th Street, Torrance, CA 90510
Model Power, 180 Smith Street, Farmingdale, NY 11735
Model Power Mfg Co., Inc., 200 5th Avenue, New York, NY 10010
Model Rectifier Corp., 200 Carter Drive, Edison, NJ 08817
Palo Imports, 184 Greenwood Avenue, Bethel, CT 06801
Permacraft Products, 9517 Jackson Street, Mentor, OH 44060
Plastruct, 1020 S. Wallace Place, City of Industry, CA 91478
Steven International, P.O. Box 126, Magnolia, NJ 08049
Super Scale Models, 200 5th Avenue, New York, NY 10010
Tyco Toys, Inc., 6000 Midlantic Drive, Mount Laurel, NJ 08054
Walthers, Inc., 5601 W. Florist Avenue, Milwaukee, WI 53218
Woodland Scenics, P.O. Box 98, Linn Creek, MO 65052

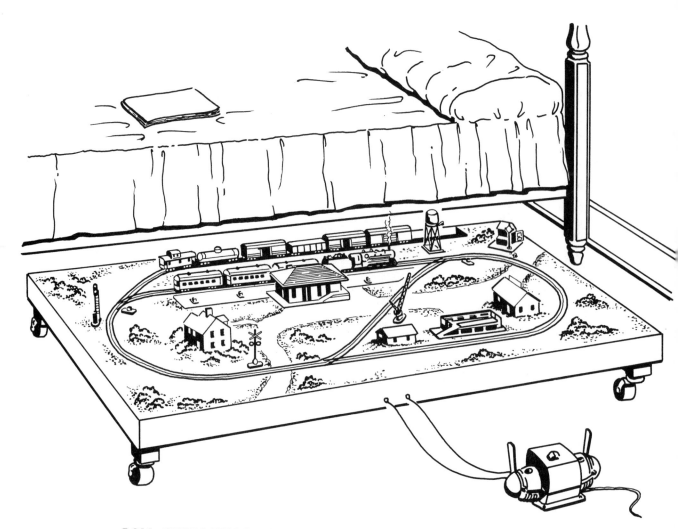

ROLL-AWAY LAYOUT: The roll-away makes an ideal first portable layout.

2
First Steps
with Model Trains

A model train layout can be built wherever there is enough space to accommodate it. A basement, den, garage, spare room or attic is a popular location. If space is limited, a layout can be erected on casters that rolls away under a bed when not in use. A fold-up layout on hinges that closes up against a wall is another suggestion if space is lacking.

Planning Your Railroad Empire

On paper, plan your train layout carefully to begin with. Draw track designs, roads, mountains, bridges and tunnels. Add areas of special interest, such as railroad yards, industrial spurs and airports. A well-planned layout will save you the time and trouble of later tearing up your track and moving it to another location. (See Chapter 6 for sample designs.)

Study track designs and choose one that is right for you, based on the size of your layout and number of trains that you will be running. Consider a two- or three-tier layout with trains running on different levels. Don't forget switches and crossovers. Make changes and "customize" the designs to your own personal liking.

Building an Operating Layout

The materials for constructing your layout can be purchased from your local lumber yard or home improvement center. Wood is graded in two main categories: *select* and *common*. Select is top-grade lumber and should be used for constructing your model train layout. Select B is perfect wood used for fine cabinet-making. Select C is excellent lumber for almost any project. Select D is a popular lumber stock, but it has imperfections, such as small knots. All select woods have smooth surfaces. Common is wood of lesser quality.

The tools needed to construct your benchwork include a saw, screwdriver, hammer, carpenter's square, wrench, drill, C-clamp and level. Power tools will help you build your layout more quickly and easily.

Construct a framework of 2×4 boards with crosspieces placed across the open center every 24 inches. Assemble the frame on a solid level surface. Drill holes through the sidepieces to meet each crosspiece. Use three 2½-inch screws at each joint. Drive the screws flush or countersink the heads. Fasten 2 legs at each corner of the frame with carriage bolts. Employ a large C-clamp to hold the legs in position on the frame while you are drilling carriage bolt holes with a ⅜-inch bit. Tap the bolts into place and tighten. The clamping action of the carriage bolts fastens the frame solidly to the legs. Add lower frame pieces for additional support. Mount them 8 inches from the bottom of each leg.

For a flat tabletop layout: Place a 4×8 sheet of plywood, ½ to ¾ inch thick, on top of the frame. A 4×8 size sound insulating board, such as Homosote, can be positioned under the plywood to reduce the noise of trains as they run on the tracks. Fasten the plywood and sound insulating board with ⅝-inch flathead screws spaced evenly along all sides.

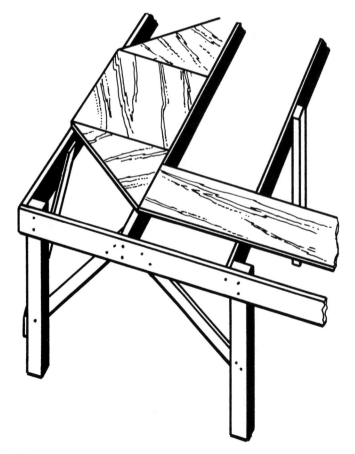

STARTING YOUR BENCHWORK

BASEMENT LAYOUT: Basements are popular locations providing space to build large permanent layouts.

For an open-grid-style layout: Cut plywood strips and sound insulating board slightly wider than your trackwork, in the design of your track plan. Use 1 × 2 pieces of lumber to raise the strips above your frame and nail in place. Open-grid layouts allow you to add scenic efforts, such as rivers and valleys, below the track level. Some layouts feature a combination of both flat tabletop and open-grid benchwork.

For larger layouts, use additional pieces of plywood and longer lengths of wood or consider building a modular layout. Several small benchwork layouts bolted together constitute a modular layout. These are convenient if you should ever have to dismantle your layout.

Once you have completed the benchwork, paint the plywood top green. Use a flat latex paint and a paint roller.

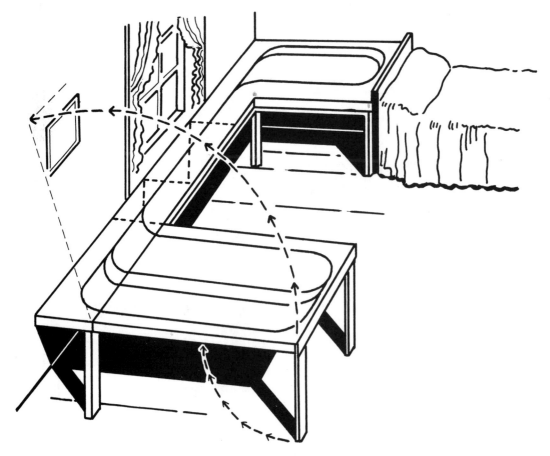

FOLD-UP LAYOUT: A layout that folds out of the way when not in use is practical when space is at a premium.

Track and Roadbed

After the paint has dried, you are ready to lay roadbed and track. Cork roadbed adds realism and helps diminish the sound of trains moving along the rails. It comes in a variety of sizes. HO size roadbed strips can be placed together to make O gauge roadbed. Use ⅛-inch nails to fasten cork roadbed to the board. Track should be nailed or screwed on the roadbed.

Most train manufacturers produce track for their brand of model trains. In addition, you can purchase track made by other companies. GarGraves is a popular flexible track for model train layouts. It has realistic wooden ties and is available in HO, O, S and Standard gauge sizes. It can be found at many hobby shops.

Switches and crossovers add variety to any track layout. Use left-handed and right-handed switches, 45-degree and 90-degree crossovers. Many switches have a non-derailing feature. When a train approaches a closed switch, it snaps open allowing the train to proceed without derailing.

Flexible cork roadbed, from Midwest Products Company, with beveled edges to resemble the ballast used on real railroads, adds realism to your layout and offers excellent sound absorption.

Mickey Mouse is the engineer of the Lionel Large Scale™ Disney Magic Express™ train set. Celebrating the thirty-fifth anniversary of Disneyland, this set features a green, red and black 0-6-0T steam locomotive with an operating smokestack, a green gondola and an illuminated caboose with Donald Duck serving as the conductor.

This N-scale Conrail diesel from Life-Like features precision details and a working headlight.

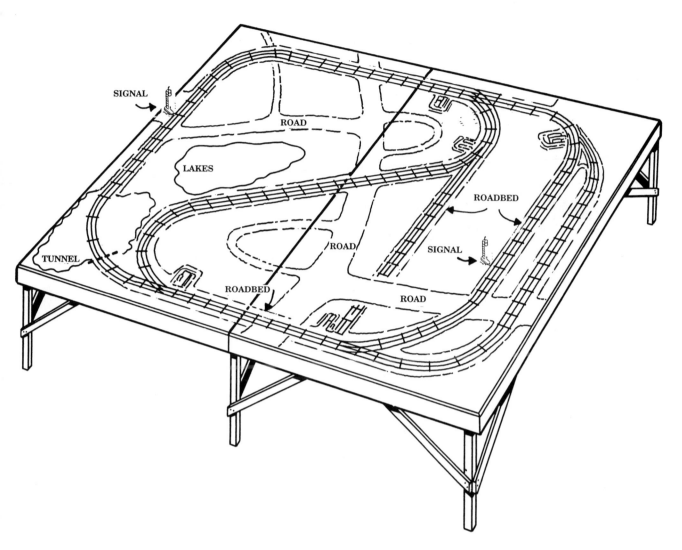

A completed layout with landscaping and scenery will provide many years of enjoyment for the model railroad enthusiast.

The orange SD-40 engine, with electronic horn, working headlight and illuminated number plates, leads the CP Rail Limited Freight Set. A silver reefer, a red boxcar, an orange gondola with a coal load, an orange Sclair hopper, a black flatcar with logs, and a yellow caboose with operating smoke and interior illumination complete this Lionel unit.

Locomotives and Rolling Stock

The main ingredient of any layout is the trains. Here the choice is immense. The range of available locomotives extends from the early General-type locomotives of the 1800s, through the powerful steam engines of the 40s and 50s, to today's modern diesels. Most trains look like and are fashioned after the prototypes on real railroads. Engines can be elaborately detailed and have realistic smoke, headlights, whistles and diesel horns.

Freight cars come in every type and road name imaginable. Gondolas and hoppers carry loads of coal and ore to the industrial areas of your

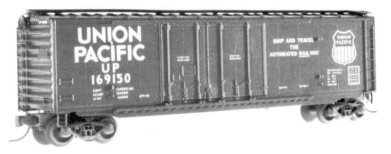

Today's modern production techniques allow manufacturers to capture fine detail, such as the workmanship on this N-scale boxcar from Kaydee Quality Products.

An alco 630 diesel locomotive with authentic Santa Fe markings from Tyco's HO gauge collection.

An alco 430 diesel from Tyco. This Virginian locomotive will add color to any HO gauge layout.

layout. Stock cars bring cattle and horses to market. Flatcars with machinery and equipment ride the rails to a local factory. Boxcars and reefers display colorful road names such as Santa Fe, Norfolk and Western, Pennsylvania and New York Central.

Echoing through narrow passages and up steep grades is the Lionel Large Scale™ Thunder Mountain Express™ set. Led by a Pennsylvania 0-4-0T steam locomotive, the two illuminated passenger cars carry silhouettes of sightseers through the peaks and valleys of the miniature world.

Passenger cars, with interior lighting, speed along the tracks carrying their silhouetted passengers to the next station. These sleek beauties include Pullmans, vistadomes and observation cars.

This wide variety of equipment allows you to select the period in history that you would like to depict on your layout—from the Old West when wood-burning locos chugged along the tracks—to today's modern diesels.

New N-scale boxcars are functional by design. Movable sliding doors are but one of the authentic features of Life-Like's new 40-foot boxcars. Both the Chessie and Ontario Northland paint schemes have a matte finish for added realism. Cars are weighted for a smooth, steady ride. Cars also feature blackened metal wheels.

The Lionel Large Scale™ Frontier Freight™, featuring bright Santa Fe markings, is led by an 0-4-0T steam locomotive with a working headlight. A flatcar with stakes, a bobber caboose, track, a U.L. approved transformer, and an engineer and fireman figure complete the set.

This five-unit Lionel train set is called the Iron Horse Freight™. It is pulled by a black die-cast metal steam locomotive with an operating headlight and smokestack. Behind the engine is a black oil tender, brown gondola with removable canisters, blue boxcar, and a red caboose. The set features an operating semaphore trackside signal, track, and a U.L. approved transformer.

The Lionel Midnight Shift™ set features a Tuscan-red Pennsylvania diesel switcher, a Tuscan-red flatcar, a gray hopper, a green gondola, and a Tuscan-red bobber caboose. Also included (but not shown) are telephone poles, a 20-piece cargo load and a mechanical crossing gate and track.

Transformers and Power Supplies

Most scale railroads are controlled by power packs that convert standard 110-volt house current to 12 volts of direct current to power the track and 16 volts of alternating current to operate the accessories. Most packages include throttle controls that start and stop the trains and control their speed. The better brands use transistorized controls. Extra throttle packs can be added if you are planning to run additional trains.

Power packs are rated in amperage. The capacity of the package should cover the number of trains running on your layout: HO scale engines use from 1 to 2 amps; N scale engines about 1 amp; O scale engines may require as many as 4 amps. In addition, allow extra amperage for accessories, such as lighted buildings.

Most tinplate layouts run on AC current. They are powered by transformers that step down standard 110-volt current to low voltage of 6–25 volts. The wattage of a transformer controls its ability to supply power. In planning your layout always calculate the capacity you will need to be sure your transformer will be sufficient. It is advisable to purchase a unit with a greater wattage than you currently need, to allow for future layout expansion.

Power packs and transformers usually feature a circuit breaker that clicks on if a short circuit should occur.

Your operating controls should be placed on a control panel. This can be a space on the edge of the layout or a separate board. A small table or desk makes an excellent place for a control panel. A slide-out drawer is another option.

Your power pack or transformer and all the switches that control tracks and accessories should be a part of the control panel.

Many hobbyists draw or paint a schematic diagram of their track plan on the control panel. Drafting tape can be used instead of paint. Switch controls are located on the diagram and correspond to the switches on the layout. Real railroads use this system to facilitate operations.

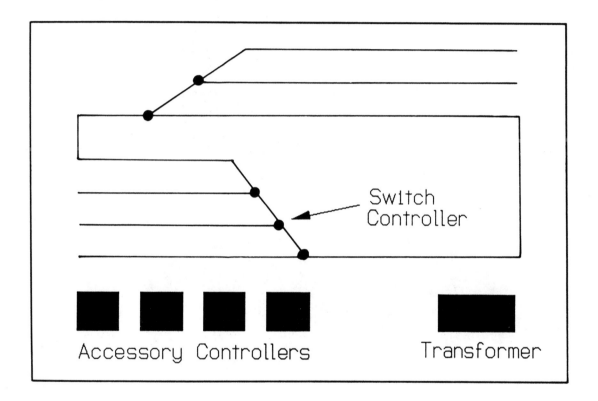

A Lionel layout, featuring the quality trains and accessories that have made Lionel a household name. Lionel has been serving the needs of model railroaders for nearly a century.

Buildings and Accessories

Stations, freight platforms, factories and houses are among many structures that can be included to bring realism to your layout. They come ready-made and in kit form. A control tower can be placed to observe the operations of your freight yard. If you have the space, a whole town or village can be created with stores, a bank, firehouse and municipal buildings. On your countryside, farmhouses, barns and miniature livestock figures will convey the perfect touch.

Miniature people and hundreds of accessories bring life to this standard-gauge layout at the Lionel Train & Seashell Museum in Sarasota, Florida.

Operating accessories add fun to the hobby. You can load and unload coal, shuttle cattle and horses into corrals, and transport cargo by magnetic crane. Signal lights, crossing gates and semaphores should be added.

Populate your layout with miniature people. Metal and plastic figures are available in all scales. They come prepainted, but also plain so that you can color them in any way you choose.

Many hobbyists build their structures from kits. This Ace Hardware Building from Model Power is ideal for a city street setting.

Hobby Tool Manufacturers

Cooper Tools, P.O. Box 30100, Raleigh, NC 27622
Dremel, 4915 21st Street, Racine, WI 53406
Heath Company, P.O. Box 1288, Benton Harbor, MI 49022
Holiday Industries, 1200 Zerega Avenue, Bronx, NY 10462
Intromark, Inc., 701 Smithfield Street, Pittsburgh, PA 15222
Life-Like Products, Inc., 1600 Union Avenue, Baltimore, MD 21211
Loew-Cornell, Inc., 563 Chestnut Avenue, Teaneck, NJ 07666
Master Woodcraft, Inc., 1 Hanson Place, Brooklyn, NY 11243
Model Power, 180 Smith Street, Farmingdale, NY 11735
Model Power Manufacturing Co., 200 5th Avenue, New York, NY 10010
Model Rectifier Corp., 200 Carter Drive, Edison, NJ 08817
Moody Tools, Inc., 48–52 Crompton Avenue, East Greenwich, RI 02818
Plastruct, 1020 S. Wallace Place, City of Industry, CA 91478
Polyfoam Products, Inc., 9420 W. Bryon Street, Schiller Park, IL 60176
Scientific Models, Inc., 340 Snyder Avenue, Berkeley Heights, NJ 07922
Skilcraft Corp., 8601 Waukegan Road, Morton Grove, IL 60053
Walthers, Inc., 5601 W. Florist Avenue, Milwaukee, WI 53218

Fairbanks-Morse coaling tower. A finely tooled stairway is but
one of the highlights of the Co-Op Elevator, an N-scale building
kit from Life-Like. Lighted for added realism, this structure also
features intricate roof and window trim, plus a chute that might
be used for coal, gravel or grain.

An HO scale Citibank building from Model Power. Structures such as this add
realism to your layout.

Many hobbyists prefer to construct their buildings from kits. A variety of kits is available, such as this Freight Terminal from Model Power in HO and N scale.

Tyco's Piggyback Loader/Unloader, available in HO gauge, comes complete with trailers, truck cab, flatcar and depot.

A Giant Operating Crane from Tyco hoists a steel girder above the tracks. This HO gauge model is one of the many accessories that you can use to provide action on your layout.

This suburban split-level home from Life-Like is one of the many highly detailed kits available to decorate your layout.

Landscaping and Scenery

Scenery is the finishing touch. You can choose from a wide variety of materials, such as artificial grass, ballast, rocks, trees and bushes. Your landscape can reflect any season of the year.

Grass and ballast should be glued to your tabletop with Ballast Cement. Trees and bushes, that come without stands, can be fastened by drilling small holes and placing the tree trunks in these holes.

Roads and highways can be painted on your tabletop surface with yellow drafting tape for the center lines. Be sure to add vehicles, road signs, miniature billboards and telephone poles. Black thread can be strung from the poles to simulate telephone lines.

The traditional method of making mountains is to first form your shapes with galvanized window screen over wooden supports, then use layers of industrial paper towels soaked in plaster over the screen. Add a cup of plaster to one quart of water and stir. Add additional cups of plaster until the mixture becomes creamy. Soak the paper towels in the plaster mix and drape them on the screen material. Use molding plaster to shape additional effects on your mountains. When dried, your mountains will be ready for painting. Use green for grassy areas, gray for rock formations and brown on other areas.

OPEN-GRID LAYOUT: An open-grid layout requires more work and planning, but allows for dynamic scenic effects.

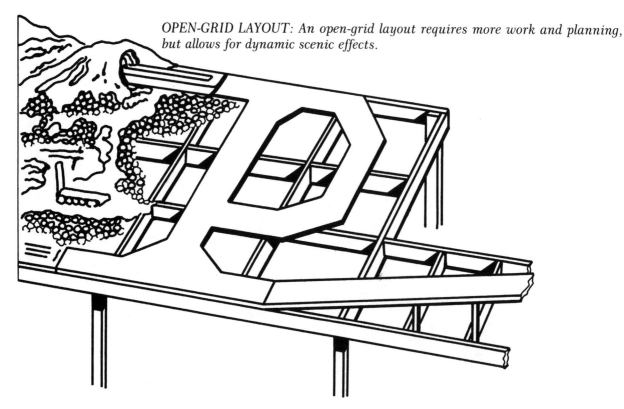

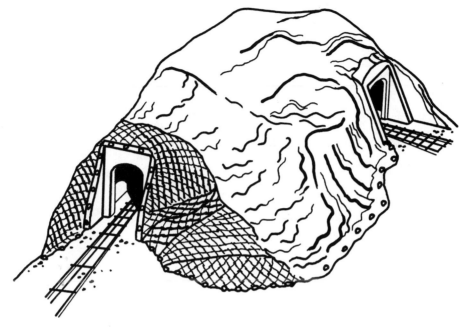

BUILDING MOUNTAINS: Realistic mountains can be designed by shaping plaster or modeling compound over standard household screen.

PERMA-SCENE, from Permacraft Products, is an easy-to-use modeling compound for sculpturing mountains, tunnels, rock formations and scenic terrains. Mix it with water and paint it when dry.

MOUNTAINS IN MINUTES is a rock-casting kit. It includes liquid polyfoam that you must pour into a latex mold shaped like a rock. When dried, the rock is ready to paint. You can mold your own rocks by painting liquid latex over real rocks and using plaster for the mold.

Having your trains run behind mountains or through tunnels adds variety to your layout. Most hobby shops carry tunnel portals for the entrances and exits of your tunnels.

The most realistic water for model train layouts is made with clear epoxy resin. You can create rivers, lakes and ponds using this substance. Make your waterbed out of molded plaster and paint it the color you desire. Make sure it is watertight as the resin will run before it hardens. Mix about 5 ounces of clear resin with an equal amount of resin hardener. Add a drop or two of blue dye or food coloring to the mixture and stir thoroughly. Pour the mixture into your waterbed until it is about ½ inch high. The resin will harden in about an hour. Wait 24 hours before adding your next layer. You can create ripples in your top layer by pulling a knife through the surface during the first hour that it is hardening. A spotlight placed

A working steamboat paddles down the river at Oglebay Park in Wheeling, West Virginia. This O gauge layout features real water.

near the surface also will cause rippling effects. It is a good idea to make a test waterway before actually placing it on your layout. Experiment with the waterbed color, resin color and ripple effects to be sure you have the desired results.

A painted sky backdrop will add depth to your layout. You can paint sky and clouds on linoleum or you can use cloud-covered wallpaper.

A model train "engineer," sitting at his control panel, schedules the movement of his trains along the many scale miles of track at Oglebay Park. This display features multilevel mountains and tunnels as well as realistic landscaping.

Operating Your Trains

It is fun to watch model trains travel around an oval of track, but even more fun to operate them like the real railroads. You can do this with even a small layout. Couple and uncouple your cars to make up different train sets. Prepare timetables and send your passenger and freight trains to their destinations, real or imaginary, through various routes on your layout. Make up waybills for your freight cars and dispatch them to industrial spurs for loading and unloading of cargo.

Plan a schedule of tasks to perform. Invite your family and friends to participate. All your "engineers" must make sure they complete their assignments and their trains are on time.

The Intermodal Crane from Lionel is a fully operational model of a 48-foot tall rolling giant from Mi-Jack® Products of Hazel Crest, Illinois. It allows the model railroader to incorporate the latest development in cargo transport into your miniaturized world. Features include forward and backward steerable drive of the entire crane, pivoting in place, turning left or right, raising and lowering of the lift carriage, lateral movement of the carriage, and opening and closing of the lift claws to accommodate all sizes of trailer.

A resurrection of an old favorite, the Lionel track-maintenance car operates on a separate spur, moving down the track until it encounters a bumper and then reversing until hitting another. It has a sign on the deck that flips with a change in direction.

Maintaining Your System

Proper maintenance will keep your layout running smoothly. Wipe your track regularly with a lint-free cloth and use a small paintbrush to dust your trains and accessories. A small vacuum cleaner can also be used. Use the vacuum carefully if you have any loose ballast or scenic material lying around. Cover your layout with a drop-cloth when it will not be in use for long periods.

The electrical sparkling, caused by trains running along the track, will eventually leave a black coating on the rails. This you can remove with a hard eraser or track-cleaning solution. Abrasive materials such as sandpaper should be avoided.

Periodically check your entire layout and benchwork for loose nails and screws. These can eventually work their way onto your track and cause a short circuit.

Lubricate your locomotives according to the manufacturer's instructions. Save the instruction sheets and warranties that are included with each item.

Buford and Roscoe pump their way down the track on this operating handcar which is new in Lionel's Large Scale™ line. Using the tools they keep on board, they can repair breakages and move merrily along.

After 47 years, the Lionel Pennsylvania 0-6-0 B-6 steam Switcher returns. Lionel has equipped the B-6 with all-new electronic RailSounds™ that are so real the Pennsylvania Switcher sounds like a real locomotive.

3
Enhancing Your Layout

Lighting Effects

Use overhead chandeliers or spotlights to brighten your layout. A fader switch on your control panel can be used to fade to dark. For something special, use black light bulbs to shine on scenery painted with fluorescent colors and get a dramatic nighttime effect.

Illuminated buildings and railroad signals add to the beauty of your night scene. Miniature lamps can be placed inside buildings that are not lighted. Block signals that change colors, a rotary beacon placed high on a hill, and microwave towers with flashing lights, all add to the realism of your layout. Add a passenger train, with illuminated cars, streaking through the night to complete your nighttime magic.

The silver, red, and blue Amtrak Passenger set from Lionel is headed up by a powerful GG-1 locomotive. Six matching aluminum passenger cars with illumination and passenger silhouettes in each window complete the train.

Using Computers and Video

The age of the microprocessor is here and computers have found their way into model railroading. Computers can be used to design your layout, control complex signal systems, aid in the scheduling of your trains, and keep track of your inventory.

Track designs can be devised with many CAD (Computer Aided Design) software programs. These programs allow you to draw both simple and complex track patterns to precise measurements and make revisions quickly and easily. You don't have to buy an expensive CAD program. Some of the simpler ones will do. AUTOSKETCH, DESIGNCAD and EASYCAD are among the popular CAD programs suitable for track design.

DESIGN YOUR OWN TRAIN is a computer software program from Abracadata. Using icons, pull-down menus and a library of pre-drawn shapes, you can build a complete layout on screen and operate up to four trains running at one time.

Timetable programs, dispatcher simulation and yard switching are available on computer software. These programs enable you to operate your layout like a real railroad.

Database software can be used to keep records of your model train inventory. These programs allow you to add as much information as you wish, sort by any category, print reports, and calculate the value of your collection.

Lionel's new RAIL SCOPE is the latest in video technology. The system includes a specially outfitted diesel locomotive with a miniature TV camera mounted inside its cab. As your train winds its way along the countryside, over bridges and into mountain tunnels, pictures from the engineer's point of view are transmitted to a television monitor located nearby.

The Lionel 4.5" TV set is offered for use with the RailScope™ engine. Using a miniature video camera mounted in the locomotive, a crisp black-and-white picture is projected onto the TV screen to give you an engineer's view of the layout as the train runs.

The yellow-and-red Dash 8-40C, in Union Pacific markings, is Lionel's replica of General Electric's advanced diesel locomotive. It features a remotely activated horn, working headlights, a flashing warning light, detailed trim, and an engineer figure at the controls. A smoking, illuminated Union Pacific caboose matches the locomotive and makes for a dazzling duo on any layout.

Adding Sound to Your System

Miniature stereo speakers that provide full high-fidelity sound can be hidden behind your mountains. Connected to a turntable, tape deck or compact disk player on your control panel, they add a new dimension to your train layout. Sound effects records, such as the ENVIRONMENTS series from Syntonic Research of New York City, will provide rain and thunder, crickets chirping in the night, and other sounds to enhance your model railroad. Or add some railroad music, like *The Orange Blossom Special*, playing as your trains speed along the tracks.

On display at the Lionel Train and Seashell Museum in Sarasota, Florida, are many prewar model trains and accessories, including the standard gauge model of a steam locomotive. Other train exhibits pictured in this book are Roadside America (page 56), Oglebay Park (pages 44, 45, and 58), San Diego Model Railroad Museum (page 57) and more Lionel (page 35).

Model Train Exhibits

You will gain many ideas from visiting commercial model train exhibits. There are a number of major exhibits scattered across the country. For a small admission fee you can witness the ultimate in model railroading. Some layouts, such as Roadside America, are spectacular in size. Others, like Oglebay Park, have distinctive features that make them unique. A river of real water with operating boats runs through Oglebay's layout. Study the track arrangements at these exhibits and the placement of buildings and accessories. Note the scenic details and special enhancements that are featured. You may be able to duplicate many of these on your own layout.

Model Train Exhibits

California

San Diego Model Railroad Museum, 1649 El Prado, San Diego CA 92101

Florida

Lionel Train & Seashell Museum, 8184 North Tamiami Trail, Sarasota, FL 34243

Whistlestop USA, P.O. Box 1, Cypress Gardens, FL 33884

Illinois

Valley View Model Railroad, 17108 Highbridge Road, Union, IL 60180

Iowa

Trainland U.S.A., Route 2, Highway 117 North, Colfax, IA 50054

New Hampshire

Klickety-Klack Railroad, P.O. Box 205, Wolfeboro Falls, NH 03896

Ohio

Railways of America, 135 South Broadway, Akron, OH 44308

Pennsylvania

Roadside America, P.O. Box 2, Shartlesville, PA 19554

Lycoming County Historical Museum, 858 West 4th Street, Williamsport, PA 17701

Toy Train Museum, P.O. Box 248, Strasburg, PA 17579

Tennessee

Chattanooga Choo-Choo, 1400 Market Street, Chattanooga, TN 37402

West Virginia

Oglebay Park, Star Route 88, Oglebay, WV 26003

Wisconsin

Park Lane Model Railroad Museum, Route 1, Box 1548, Reedsburg, WI 53959

A village square at Roadside America in Shartlesville, Pennsylvania. This O gauge layout is one of the largest in the United States and features toy trains running on more than 2000 feet of track.

Computer Programs for Model Railroads

Bryan Consulting Services, 2303 W. Reading Street, Tulsa, OK 74127
Data Blocks, 579 Snowhill Road, Alama, GA 30411
Medprof, Inc., P.O. Box 440486, Aurora, CO 80044
Mil-Scale Products, P.O. Box 13612, Wauwatosa, WI 53213
Railway Educational Bureau, 1809 Capitol Avenue, Omaha, NE 68102
TCI, 22 Executive Park, Irvine, CA 92714

The Lionelville™ Circus Special set, headed up by an 1850's-style 4-4-0 steam loco-motive. This colorful five-unit set also includes a Lionelville Circus tender, an oper-ating animated car featuring clowns in a chase, an operating elephant car and a lighted caboose.

Modern railroading is depicted with this Silver Spike™ set from Lionel. Two sleek silver, blue, and red FA-1 diesel engines pull this train which also includes a matching combo car, vistadome car, and an observation car. An oval track and U.L. approved transformer complete the set.

Lionel's Large Scale™ wooden car kits are made from American alder wood. Ready for finishing and assembly are a 1936 Ford pickup, a 1926 Ford Model A coupe, and a 1936 Ford "Woody" station wagon, all to be used to give a real-life look to your station area.

The Lionel Nickel Plate Special™ is led by a black die-cast metal steam locomotive with an operating headlight and puffing smokestack. This engine is followed by a black tender with steam sound effects, yellow boxcar, black gondola with canisters, gray hopper, and a red caboose. Featured in this set are an operating crossing gate and trackside accessories.

A real water river flows alongside a toy town at the 1200-square-foot train layout at Oglebay Park in Wheeling, West Virginia.

A Western scene of the early 1950's is depicted on this HO scale model train layout at the San Diego Model Railroad Museum.

4
Collecting Toy Trains

Train collecting is another facet of the hobby. You will always be delighted when adding a new piece to your collection. Antique trains are still available today and displayed for sale at train shows throughout the country. The value of many collectibles has increased dramatically through the

A very busy railroad station featuring Marklin trains and accessories.

years. Model trains made over the years by Lionel are the most popular among collectors. American Flyer and Ives are also in demand.

The condition of an item plays an important part in estimating its value. Some collectors will not accept items unless they are in Like New or Mint condition, but most will draw the line at Excellent or Very Good. The new collector may find it difficult to grade trains accurately at first. Experience is the best teacher. As you move along, you will soon develop an eye for assessing minor and major defects at a glance.

Many collectors have adopted the following definitions for grading collectible toy trains: MINT—Brand-new, absolutely free of defects, original and unused. LIKE NEW—Original condition, free of any scratches or blemishes, very little sign of use. EXCELLENT—Minor scratches or blemishes, exceptionally clean with no dents or rust, only slight sign of use. VERY GOOD—Some scratches, exceptionally clean, no dents or rust, some sign of use. GOOD—Scratches, small dents, dirty, considerable sign of use. FAIR—Well scratched, chipped, dented or rusted condition, in need of repair. POOR—Junk condition, valued only for usable parts, incomplete or unsuitable for collection purposes.

Many collectors view model trains as an investment. They display their trains on shelves or behind glass. There are collectors in the United States who have "train rooms" with shelves of trains worth many thousands of dollars.

Train Clubs and Organizations

Your local hobby shop should be able to direct you to train clubs in your area. These clubs provide meeting places for fellow collectors to get together and talk about their hobby. Many clubs have operating layouts. Individual members usually contribute their time and talent to the club layout construction and bring their trains to run.

National organizations augment model train collecting and keep their members informed of news about the hobby. The Train Collectors Association was the first organization devoted exclusively to collectors of toy trains. It has regional divisions throughout the United States and manages a train museum in Strasburg, Pennsylvania.

Lionel Trains has its own Lionel Railroader Club. It publishes a newsletter, *The Inside Track*, that informs its members of special offers and new Lionel products.

Shows and Conventions

Train meets are held throughout the year in many parts of the United States. Here collectors buy, sell and trade their train-related wares. As a collector, you will make new friends at these shows who share your interest in the hobby.

The major train organizations hold national conventions in different parts of the country. These annual conventions often feature seminars, lectures and workshops on various aspects of the hobby.

Magazines and Newsletters

Model train magazines provide up-to-date information on the hobby. The major magazines contain useful articles on model building and operating your layout. They publish layout photos, from which you can gather ideas, and listings of model train stores throughout the United States. Notices of upcoming train shows are also included. The variety of advertisements in these magazines will keep you informed of the newest products available in the hobby.

Train organizations publish newsletters containing useful information for their members. They also distribute directories of their membership. Many members are happy to have people visit and view their layouts or collections.

Model Train Organizations

Lionel Collectors Club of America, P.O. Box 479, LaSalle, IL 61301
Lionel Operating Train Society, 7408 138th Place NE, Redmond, WA 98052
Lionel Railroader Club, P.O. Box 748, Mount Clemens, MI 48043
Marklin Club, P.O. Box 795, Elm Grove, WI 53122
Model Railroad Industry Association, P.O. Box 28129, Denver, CO 80228
National Association of S Gaugers, 709 Reedy Circle, Bel Air, MD 21014
National Model Railroad Association, P.O. Box 1328, Station C, Canton, OH 44708
Teen Association of Model Railroaders, 1028 Whaley Road, New Carlisle, OH 45344
Toy Train Operating Society, 25 West Walnut Street, Suite 408, Pasadena, CA 91103
Train Collectors Association, P.O. Box 248, Strasburg, PA 17579

Model Train Magazines

Classic Toy Trains, P.O. Box 1612, Waukesha, WI 53187
Garden Railways Magazine, P.O. Box 61461, Denver, CO 80206
Model Railroader, 1027 North 7th Street, Milwaukee, WI 53233
Model Railroading, 2854 Larimer Street, Denver, CO 80205
O Scale Railroading, P.O. Box 239, Nazareth, PA 18064
Prototype Modeler, P.O. Box 7032, Fairfax Station, VA 22039
Railroad Model Craftsman, P.O. Box 700, Newton, NJ 07860

All aboard! Passengers get ready to board an old-time railroad train in Strasburg, Pennsylvania.

5

Train Museums and Tourist Railroads

Studying the prototypes and railroad history will involve you in the hobby—and may influence your decisions in train collecting and layout planning.

Although the age of steam has passed us by, the glorious locomotives of this era live on in the museums and tourist railroads of the U.S. and Canada. Plan to visit one in your area or on your next vacation. Ride in an old-time coach pulled by a massive steam turbine. Hear the sounds and smell the odors of these bygone giants. Don't forget to bring along

A passenger train from the Golden Age of Steam speeds along the rails at the Steamtown National Historic Site in Scranton, Pennsylvania.

your camera. Experience real railroading and bring this education back home to your model railroad empire.

Some tourist railroads have only one or two locomotives, while others have many. Most charge fares for the train rides and offer parking and restaurant facilities. Picnic areas and nearby lodging are sometimes available. It is a good idea to check ahead and see what each has to offer. As most of the operations are outdoors, they are open only during the warm-weather months.

On the tracks of the Strasburg Rail Road, the engineer gets ready to stop the train so the passengers can get off and take photographs.

Train Museums

Alaska
Museum of Alaska Transportation and Industry, P.O. Box 909, Palmer, AK 99645

California
California State Railroad Museum, 111 I Street, Sacramento, CA 95814
Laws Railroad Museum, P.O. Box 363, Bishop, CA 93514
Pacific Southwest Railway Museum, 4695 Railroad Avenue, La Mesa, CA 92041
Lomita Railroad Museum, 2135–37 250th Street West, Lomita, CA 90717
Orange Empire Railway Museum, P.O. Box 548, Perris, CA 92370
Portola Railroad Museum, P.O. Box 8, Portola, CA 96122
Western Railway Museum, P.O. Box 3694, San Francisco, CA 94119

Visitors to Great American in Santa Clara, California, can ride a scenic railway through this 100-acre theme park.

Colorado
Colorado Railroad Museum, P.O. Box 10, Golden, CO 80402
Forney Transportation Museum, 1416 Platte Street, Denver, CO 80202

Connecticut
Connecticut Valley Railroad Museum, P.O. Box 97, Essex, CT 06426

District of Columbia
Smithsonian Institution, Washington, DC 20560

Florida
Gold Coast Railroad Museum, 12450 SW 152nd Street, Miami, FL 33177

Georgia
Southeastern Railway Museum, P.O. Box 13132, Atlanta, GA 30324

Illinois
Illinois Railway Museum, P.O. Box 431, Union, IL 60180
Monticello Railway Museum, P.O. Box 401, Monticello, IL 61856

Indiana
Indiana Railway Museum, P.O. Box 150, French Lick, IN 47432
Indiana Transportation Museum, P.O. Box 83, Noblesville, IN 45060

Kentucky
Bluegrass Railroad Museum, P.O. Box 1711, Lexington, KY 40592
Kentucky Railway Museum, P.O. Box 22764, Louisville, KY 40222

Louisiana
Louisiana State Railroad Museum, P.O. Box 1835, Kenner, LA 70063

Maryland
B&O Railroad Museum, 901 West Pratt Street, Baltimore, MD 21223

Massachusetts
Berkshire Scenic Railway Museum, P.O. Box 298, Lee, MA 01238

Michigan
Henry Ford Museum, P.O. Box 1970, Dearborn, MI 49121
Michigan Transit Museum, P.O. Box 12, Fraser, MI 48026

Minnesota
Lake Superior Museum of Transportation, 506 West Michigan Street, Duluth, MN 55802
Minnesota Transportation Museum, P.O. Box 1796, St. Paul, MN 55101

Mississippi
Casey Jones Museum, P.O. Box 605, Vaughan, MS 39179

Missouri
Frisco Railroad Museum, P.O. Box 276, Ash Grove, MO 65604
National Museum of Transport, 3015 Barrett Station Road, St. Louis, MO 63122

Nebraska
Union Pacific Historical Museum, 1416 Dodge Street, Omaha, NE 68179

Nevada
Nevada Northern Railway Museum, P.O. Box 40, East Ely, NV 89315
Nevada State Railroad Museum, Capital Complex, Carson City, NV 89710

New Jersey
New Jersey Museum of Transportation, P.O. Box 622, Farmingdale, NJ 07727
Whippany Railway Museum, P.O. Box 16, Whippany, NJ 07981

New York
Martisco Station Museum, P.O. Box 229, Marcellus, NY 13108
New York Museum of Transportation, P.O. Box 136, West Henrietta, NY 14586

Oatka Depot Railroad Museum, P.O. Box 664, Rochester, NY 14603
Salamanca Rail Museum, 170 Main Street, Salamanca, NY 14779

North Carolina

Wilmington Railroad Museum, 501 Nutt Street, Wilmington, NC 28401

Ohio

Conneaut Railroad Museum, P.O. Box 643, Conneaut, OH 44030
Northern Ohio Railway Museum, P.O. Box 29265, Cleveland, OH 44129
Mad River & NKP Railroad Museum, P.O. Box 42, Bellevue, OH 44811
Ohio Railway Museum, P.O. Box 171, Worthington, OH 43085

Oklahoma

Cimarron Valley Railroad Museum, P.O. Box 844, Cushing, OK 74023
Oklahoma Transportation Museum, 1313 West Britton Road, Oklahoma
City, OK 73114

Pennsylvania

Franklin Institute Science Museum, 20th Street & The Parkway, Phila-
delphia, PA 19103
Lake Shore Railway Museum, P.O. Box 571, North East, PA 16426
Railroad Museum of Pennsylvania, P.O. Box 15, Strasburg, PA 17579
Railroaders Memorial Museum, 1300 9th Avenue, Altoona, PA 16602

Tennessee

Casey Jones Home and Railroad Museum, Casey Jones Village, Jackson,
TN 38305
Cowan Railroad Museum, P.O. Box 53, Cowan, TN 37318
Tennessee Valley Railroad Museum, 4119 Cromwell Road, Chattanooga,
TN 37421

Texas

Age of Steam Railroad Museum, P.O. Box 26369, Dallas, TX 75226
Texas Transportation Museum, 11731 Wetmore Road, San Antonio, TX
78427
The Railroad Museum, 123 Rosenberg Avenue, Galveston, TX 77550

Utah

Union Station, 2501 Wall Avenue, Ogden, UT 84401

Vermont

Shelburne Museum, Shelburne, VT 05482

Virginia

Virginia Museum of Transportation, 303 Norfolk Avenue, Roanoke, VA
24011

Wisconsin

Mid-Continent Railway Museum, P.O. Box 55, North Freedom, WI 53951
Rail America National Railroad Museum, 2285 South Broadway, Green
Bay, WI 54304

A mighty steam engine journeys through the countryside at the Strasburg Rail Road in Strasburg, Pennsylvania.

Tourist Railroads

Arkansas
Eureka Springs & North Arkansas Railway, P.O. Box 310, Eureka Springs, AR 72632
Reader Railroad, P.O. Box 9, Malvern, AR 72104

California
Calico & Odessa Railroad, P.O. Box 638, Yermo, CA 92398
California Western Railroad, P.O. Box 907, Fort Bragg, CA 95437
Disneyland Railroad, 1313 Harbor Boulevard, Anaheim, CA 92803
Folsom Valley Railway, P.O. Box 261, El Dorado, CA 95623
Ghost Town & Calico Railroad, 8039 Beach Boulevard, Buena Park, CA 90620
Great American Scenic Railway, P.O. Box 1776, Santa Clara, CA 95052
Niles Canyon Railway, P.O. Box 2247, Niles Station, Fremont, CA 94536

Riding through Pennsylvania's countryside on the Strasburg Railroad.

Roaring Camp & Big Trees Railroad, P.O. Box 1, Felton, CA 95018
Santa Cruz, Big Trees & Pacific Railway, P.O. Box 1, Felton, CA 95018
Sonoma Train Town Railroad, P.O. Box 656, Sonoma, CA 95476
Travel Town Railroad, 115 South Victory Boulevard, Burbank, CA 91502
Yosemite Mountain–Sugar Pine Railroad, 56001 Highway 41, Fish Camp, CA 93623
Yreka Western Railroad, 300 East Miner Street, Yreka, CA 96097

Colorado

Cadillac & Lake City Railway, 121 East Pikes Peak Avenue, Colorado Springs, CO 80903
Cripple Creek and Victor Railroad, P.O. Box 459, Cripple Creek, CO 80813
Durango & Silverton Railroad, 479 Main Avenue, Durango, CO 81301
Georgetown Loop Railroad, P.O. Box 217, Georgetown, CO 80444
High Country Railroad, 1540 Routt Street, Lakewood, CO 80215
Manitou & Pikes Peak Railway, P.O. Box 1329, Colorado Springs, CO 80901
Royal Gorge Scenic Railway, P.O. Box 1387, Canon City, CO 81212

Connecticut
Valley Railroad, P.O. Box 452, Essex, CT 06426

Delaware
Wilmington & Western Railroad, P.O. Box 5787, Wilmington, DE 19808

Florida
Disney World Railroad, P.O. Box 10000, Lake Buena Vista, FL 32830

Georgia
Hart County Scenic Railway, P.O. Box 429, Hartwell, GA 30643
New Georgia Railroad, 1 Martin Luther King Drive, Atlanta, GA 30334

Hawaii
Lahaina Kaanapali & Pacific Railroad, P.O. Box 816, Lahaina, HI 96761

Illinois
Silver Creek & Stephenson Railroad, P.O. Box 255, Freeport, IL 61032

Indiana
Little River Railroad, P.O. Box 178, Angola, IN 46703
Whitewater Valley Railroad, P.O. Box 406, Connersville, IN 47331

Iowa
Boone & Scenic Valley Railroad, P.O. Box 603, Boone, IA 50036
Midwest Central Railroad, Threshers Road, Mt. Pleasant, IA 52641
Star Clipper Dinner Train, P.O. Box 1917, Waterloo, IA 50704

Kentucky
Big South Fork Scenic Railway, P.O. Box 248, Stearns, KY 42647

Maine
Belfast & Moosehead Lake Railroad, 11 Water Street, Belfast, ME 04915

Maryland
Allegany Central Railroad, Canal Street, Cumberland, MD 21502
Maryland Midland Railway, P.O. Box A, Union Bridge, MD 21791

Massachusetts
Cape Cod & Hyannis Railroad, 252 Main Street, Hyannis, MA 02601
Edaville Railroad, P.O. Box 7, South Carver, MA 02366
Pioneer Valley Railroad, 221 Appleton Street, Holyoke, MA 01040
Providence & Worcester Railroad, P.O. Box 1188, Worcester, MA 01601

Michigan
Coe Rail, 840 North Pontiac Trail, Walled Lake, MI 48088
Huckleberry Railroad, 5055 Branch Street, Flint, MI 48506
Junction Valley Railroad, 7065 Dixie Highway, Bridgeport, MI 48722
Leelanau Scenic Railroad, 9945 Carter Road, Traverse City, MI 49684
South Michigan Railroad, P.O. Box 434, Clinton, MI 49236
Toonerville Trolley, 115 East Avenue A, Newberry, MI 49868

Minnesota
Minnesota Zephyr Limited, P.O. Box 573, Stillwater, MN 55082

Missouri

St. Louis & Chain of Rocks Railroad, 3422 Osage Street, St. Louis, MO 63118

St. Louis, Iron Mountain & Southern, P.O. Box 244, Jackson, MO 63755

Wabash, Frisco & Pacific, 1569 Ville Angela Lane, Hazelwood, MO 63042

Montana

Neversweat & Washoe Railroad, 305 West Mercury, Butte, MT 59701

Nebraska

Fremont & Elkhorn Valley Railroad, P.O. Box 939, Fremont, NE 68025

Nevada

Virginia & Truckee Railroad, P.O. Box 467, Virginia City, NV 89440

New Hampshire

Conway Scenic Railroad, P.O. Box 947, North Conway, NH 03860

Mt. Washington Cog Railway, P.O. Box 932, Littleton, NH 03561

White Mountain Central Railroad, P.O. Box 1, Lincoln, NH 03251

Winnipesaukee Railroad, RFD 4, Box 317, Meredith, NH 03253

New Jersey

Black River & Western Railroad, P.O. Box 200, Ringoes, NJ 08551

New Mexico

Cumbres & Toltec Scenic Railroad, P.O. Box 789, Chama, NM 87520

New York

Arcade & Attica Railroad, 278 Main Street, Arcade, NY 14009

Catskill Mountain Railroad, P.O. Box 46, Shokan, NY 12481

Delaware & Ulster Rail Ride, P.O. Box 243, Stamford, NY 12167

Tioga Central, RD 4, Box 4240, Owego, NY 13827

North Carolina

New Hope Valley Railway, P.O. Box 83, New Hill, NC 27562

Tweetsie Railroad, P.O. Box 388, Blowing Rock, NC 28605

Ohio

Buckeye Central Scenic Railroad, P.O. Box 242, Newark, OH 43055

Hocking Valley Scenic Railway, P.O. Box 427, Nelsonville, OH 45764

Indiana & Ohio Railroad, 11020 Reading Road, Cincinnati, OH 45241

Oregon

Oregon Pacific & Eastern Railway, P.O. Box 565, Cottage Grove, OR 97424

Sumpter Valley Railroad, P.O. Box 389, Baker, OR 97814

Pennsylvania

Blue Mountain & Reading Railroad, P.O. Box 425, Hamburg, PA 19526

East Broad Top Railroad, Rockhill Furnace, PA 17249

Gettysburg Railroad, P.O. Box 1267, Gettysburg, PA 17325

New Hope Steam Railway, P.O. Box 612, Huntington Valley, PA 19006

Oil Creek & Titusville Railroad, P.O. Box 68, Oil City, PA 16301

Passengers take a scenic ride through Vermont's countryside on the Green Mountain Railroad.

Rail Tours, P.O. Box 285, Jim Thorpe, PA 18229
Steamtown USA, P.O. Box F, Scranton, PA 18501
Stewartstown Railroad, P.O. Box 155, Stewartstown, PA 17363
Stourbridge Line Rail Excursions, 742 Main Street, Honesdale, PA 18431
Strasburg Rail Road, P.O. Box 96, Strasburg, PA 17579
Wanamaker, Kempton & Southern, P.O. Box 24, Kempton, PA 19529
West Shore Railroad, RD 3, Box 155, Lewisburg, PA 17837

Rhode Island
Old Colony & Newport Railway, P.O. Box 343, Newport, RI 02840

South Dakota
Black Hills Central Railroad, P.O. Box 1880, Hill City, SD 57745

Texas
Jefferson & Cypress Bayou Railroad, P.O. Drawer A, Jefferson, TX 75657
Six Flags Railroad, P.O. Box 191, Arlington, TX 76004
Texas Mexican Railway, P.O. Box 419, Laredo, TX 78042

Utah
Heber Creeper, P.O. Box 103, Heber City, UT 84032

Vermont
Green Mountain Railroad, P.O. Box 498, Bellows Falls, VT 05101
Lamoille Valley Railroad, Stafford Avenue, Morrisville, VT 05661

Washington
Anacortes Railway, 387 Campbell Lake Road, Anacortes, WA 98221
Lake Whatcom Railway, P.O. Box 91, Acme, WA 98220
Mount Rainier Scenic Railroad, P.O. Box 921, Elbe WA 98330
Puget Sound & Snoqualmie Valley Railroad, P.O. Box 459, Snoqualmie, WA 98065

West Virginia
Cass Scenic Railroad, P.O. Box 107, Cass, WV 24927

Wisconsin
Kettle Moraine Railway, P.O. Box 247, North Lake, WI 53064
Laona & Northern Railway, Route 1, Laona, WI 54541
Scenic Rail Dining, 11340 West Brown Deer Road, Milwaukee, WI 53224

Railroad Theme Parks

Arizona
McCormick Railroad Park, 7301 East Indian Bend Road, Scottsdale, AZ 85253

Maine
Boothbay Railway Village, P.O. Box 123, Boothbay, ME 04537
Sandy River Railroad Park, P.O. Box 8, Phillips, ME 04966

Minnesota
Ironworld USA, P.O. Box 392, Chisholm, MN 55719

North Dakota
Bonanzaville USA, P.O. Box 719, West Fargo, ND 85078

Texas
Texas State Railroad Historical Park, P.O. Box 39, Rusk, TX 75785

Utah
Golden Spike National Historic Site, P.O. Box W, Brigham City, UT 84032

Lionel celebrated 90 years of operation in 1990 and marks the occasion with the introduction of the 90th Anniversary train set. It features a powerful GP-9 diesel engine with the realistic RailSounds™ system, operating headlights, illuminated cab and number plates, five boxcars that vividly recall the important moments in the history of Lionel and a bay window caboose that carries the theme, "And the Legend Lives On."

6

History of Model Trains

Model trains date back to the middle 1800s when tin locomotives with clockwork mechanisms delighted youngsters by running across the floor. In addition, model locomotives with small alcohol burners propelled by live steam were available from European manufacturers. These grew to be unpopular when parents feared they would be dangerous to their children.

Resurrected from the 1930's, the Blue Comet takes to the Lionel rails again this year. Featured in the Classics Line, this train includes a brilliant two-tone blue locomotive with an operating red firebox glow, an operating headlight, Rail-Sounds™ and three illuminated Pullman cars all named after comets.

The Lionel Lines #44E Freight Special replicates an "O" Gauge classic offered by Lionel from the prewar days of the 20's and 30's. With a motor designed just like the original, the #44E is a tough hauler with operating headlights, and a shiny baked enamel finish. It is followed by a hopper, a working searchlight car, a boxcar, and a center-cupola caboose, which all carry the Lionel Lines markings.

Toward the end of the nineteenth century, many model trains were made of cast-iron and wood. While most of these were wind-up or pull toys, the age of electric trains was not far away. As early as 1896, the Carlisle and Finch Company of Cincinnati, Ohio, was busy making electric trolley cars and trains in 2-inch gauge. Other companies soon followed suit. The Knapp Electric and Novelty Company of New York, and the Voltamp Electric Manufacturing Company of Baltimore, Maryland, were early producers of 2-inch gauge electric trains. European companies, such as Marklin, Bing and Hornby, also offered competition with their superb models.

Lionel Trains

In 1900, a young inventor named Joshua Lionel Cowen set up shop in New York City and began producing his first products. The Lionel Manufacturing Company produced 2⅞-inch gauge trolleys and motorized cars. In 1906, Lionel ceased its 2⅞-inch gauge items and introduced a standard gauge line of electronic trains with the first center rail electric track ever produced in the United States. Lionel added an O-gauge line in 1915.

In 1918 the firm was incorporated as The Lionel Corporation. During the 1920s and 1930s the company produced many items that are highly prized by today's collectors. During World War II, Lionel turned its facilities to the production of war materials.

During the postwar period, Lionel produced its greatest variety of trains

From the 1930's, the Lionel 384E, 2-4-0 steam locomotive and tender feature a two-tone gray finish with red striping. It has die-cast metal construction, an operating headlight and whistle, and a Bild-A-Loco™ motor. Four cars follow the 384E, including a cattle car with opening doors, a working searchlight car, a gondola, and an illuminated caboose—everything a prewar buff could want in a model train.

The Scale Hudson locomotive was first introduced by Lionel in 1937. For Lionel's 90th Anniversary, the Hudson is back, with a bolt-for-bolt reproduction of the real-life 4-6-4 locomotive. The best operating features of any Lionel locomotive are standard equipment on the #1-700E Scale Hudson. It even features Rail-Sounds™, recreating actual locomotive sounds of a tolling bell, hissing steam chuff and steam release, as well as a haunting steam whistle.

and accessories and became the largest toy company in the United States. After retiring in the late 1950s, Joshua Lionel Cowen died on September 8, 1965. This pioneer in model railroading had devoted his life to the production of toy trains and had made Lionel a household name.

During the 1960s, the Lionel company began to diversify into other areas. The company's train production operations were licensed to General Mills in 1970. Lionel Trains were produced under the General Mills banner until 1986 when the company was sold to Richard P. Kughn, a longtime collector. Under its new management, Lionel Trains, Inc. continues to produce the trains that made the company famous for almost a century.

The newest additions to Lionel's RailScope™ engines are the S Gauge, American Flyer® PA-1 diesel locomotives. This RailScope engine has a miniature video camera mounted inside. This allows the model train operator to take a trip into a world never seen before: the world of the Lionel train.

American Flyer

The Edmonds-Metzel Manufacturing Company started its "American Flyer" line of clockwork trains in 1907. In 1910, the company changed its name to the American Flyer Manufacturing Company. The firm began production on O-gauge electric trains in 1918 and introduced its standard gauge line in 1925.

American Flyer was sold to the A.C. Gilbert Company of New Haven, Connecticut, in 1938. After World War II, the company discontinued its previous lines and introduced a new two-rail S-gauge system. This system proved to be very popular among toy train enthusiasts.

Alfred Carlton Gilbert died in 1961 and, soon after, his company was bought by the Wrather Corporation, a California holding company. In 1966, the American Flyer line was sold to its chief competitor, the Lionel Corporation.

Today, Lionel has brought back the American Flyer line for the delight of S-gauge collectors everywhere.

Ives Trains

The history of Ives dates back to the 1860s when Edward Ives started a small business in Bridgeport, Connecticut, and began manufacturing toys and clockwork trains. By the turn of the century, the Ives Manufacturing Company had gained much prestige in the toy industry.

In 1900, a fire destroyed the Ives plant, but the company rose from the ashes and, despite competition from Lionel, American Flyer, and other toy train manufacturers, grew to become one of the leading toy makers of its time. Ives led the way in the early development of toy trains and was one of the first to electrify its line.

After the death of Edward Ives, his son, Harry, took control of the company and continued in his father's footsteps. Ives 1-gauge trains began production in 1904 followed by O-gauge in 1910. Ives discontinued its 1-gauge line in 1920 and introduced standard gauge in 1921, which it called wide gauge. The firm continued to manufacture high-quality toys and trains until 1932.

The Depression years of the 1930s took their toll. Ives went out of business and was bought by Lionel and American Flyer. American Flyer later sold its interest to Lionel which soon discontinued the Ives line.

The Ives motto was, "Ives Toys Make Happy Boys." Harry Ives died in 1936 never knowing that, more than 50 years in the future, his "toys" would be prized by collectors around the world.

The White Pass diesel from LGB. Fans looking for the power of a modern diesel locomotive will find a wide range of LGB locos for their needs. LGB trains can be run both indoors and outdoors in all kinds of weather.

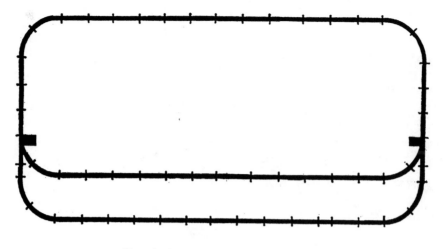

Simple Loop with Switch Track

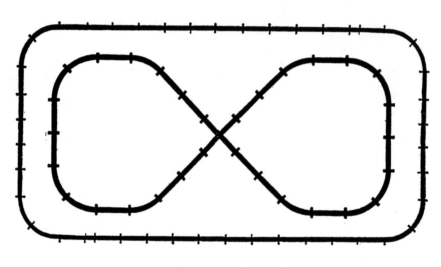

Loop with Inside Figure Eight

7
Track Layout Designs

A well-designed layout should include not only the facilities for operating your trains like the real railroads, but also the necessary ingredients for entertainment, such as switching trains to different tracks, reversing direction and operating several trains at one time.

This can be accomplished by taking a basic oval of track and adding switches, sidings and reverse loops. Use passenger and freight stations to give your trains destination and freight yards to make up different sets of rolling stock. Place industrial spurs on various portions of your layout with operating accessories for loading and unloading cargo.

One of the most enjoyable aspects of model railroading is the planning of your track patterns. This is where you will put your imagination to work. So relax, put on your engineer's thinking cap and have fun.

Diesel locomotives are the workhorses that pull the rolling stock on today's railroads. Model diesels such as these in N-scale from Life-Like are available in many colors and road names.

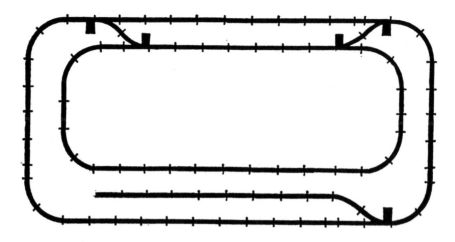

Loop with Inside Connecting Loop and Siding

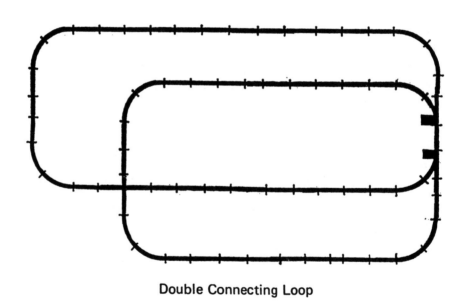

Double Connecting Loop

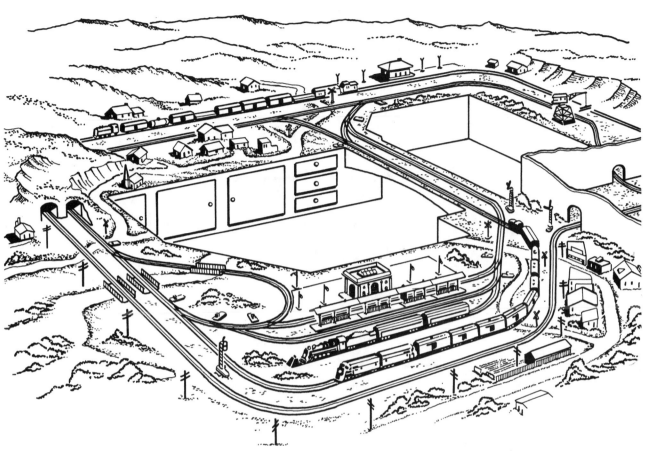

If space permits, complex track plans can be created to add variety to the move-
ments of your trains.

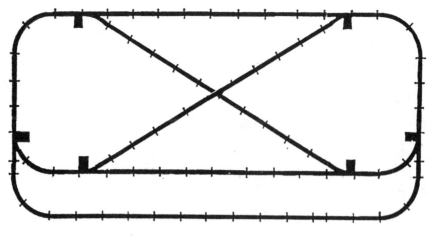

Reversing Loop and Switch Track

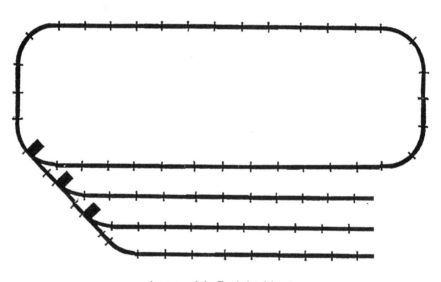

Loop with Freight Yard

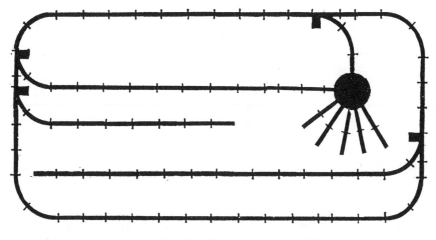

Loop with Engine Turntable and Sidings

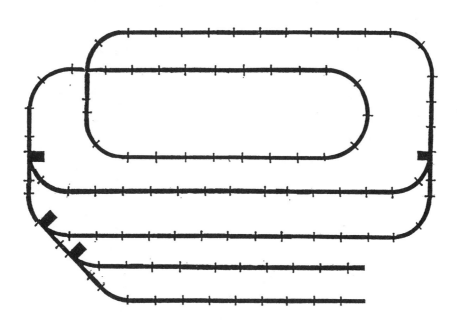

Loop with Extra Curves, Switch Track and Sidings

The Gold Rush Special™ set from Lionel is a complete three-unit Large Scale™ train bearing Denver and Rio Grande markings. It is headed up by an 0-6-0T wood-burning locomotive with an engineer figure, and is followed by an old-style gondola, and a lighted caboose. The set is complete with track and a U.L. approved transformer.

8
Dictionary of Model Railroad Terms

Like most hobbies, model railroading has a terminology all its own. Learning these words and their meanings will help you to get involved in the hobby.

Some words, such as "engineer," will be familiar to you. Others, such as "fishplate," will be new. There are also words, such as "nose," that have meanings completely different from what you would expect.

Alternating Current—standard household current that reverses direction of flow at regular intervals.

Amp—as unit of measure for electrical strength; full name is ampere.

Automatic Coupler—coupler that works automatically by remote control.

Baggage Car—railroad car used for carrying passengers' baggage.

Ballast—material placed on the track to hold ties in place.

Block—a segment of track that is controlled as a unit.

Block Signal—a railway signal that controls a block of track.

Boiler—part of a steam locomotive that produces steam and runs the engine.

Boxcar—covered freight car used for hauling cargo.

Cab—locomotive enclosure that shelters the engineer.

Caboose—last car in a freight train used for housing the conductor and other crew members.

Catenary—cable that contains power in an overhead electrification system.

Circuit Breaker—a switch that automatically interrupts the electrical current if an overload occurs.

Conductor—member of a train crew who is in charge of the train while it is not moving.

Coupler—device for connecting railroad cars together. Both manual and automatic couplers are used.

Crossing—an intersection between tracks.

Crossover—junction between two parallel tracks.

Current—the flow of electricity through a circuit.

Diesel—locomotive with a compression ignition, internal combustion engine.

Direct Current—electrical current that flows in one direction continuously.

Drawbar—device for connecting a steam locomotive with its tender.

Drive Wheels—the powered wheels of a locomotive.

Embankment—hill or ridge of earth to elevate the natural ground level.

Engineer—member of a train crew in charge of the train while it is in motion.

E-Unit—a reversing mechanism in model locomotives.

Firebox—part of a steam locomotive boiler where the combustion of fuel takes place.

Fishplate—metal piece used for connecting lengths of rail together.

Flange—projecting edge or rim of a wheel that guides the wheel along the tracks.

Flatcar—a freight car used for carrying items that can be tied down.

Footplate—cab floor of a steam locomotive.

Pizza Hut from Tyco's contemporary series of model kits. Finished in authentic colors, this HO gauge building is one of the many kits available from Tyco.

Gauge—the distance between the running rails of a track.

Gondola—a freight car used for transporting coal and ore.

Grade Crossing—an intersection between railway tracks and a road or highway.

Hopper—freight car that unloads its cargo through the floor. Hoppers may be covered or uncovered.

Locomotive—engine that pulls a train. Locomotives can be steam, diesel or electrically powered.

Loop—a continuous circular arrangement of track.

Narrow Gauge—railroad track of smaller than the standard gauge.

Nose—the front end of a locomotive.

Observation car—passenger car placed at the rear of the train with windows situated to give passengers a maximum view of the scenery.

Pantograph—a collapsible frame on the roof of an electric engine connecting it to an overhead catenary system.

Piggyback Car—a flat car designed to hold highway trailers.

Prototype—the real-life train from which a model is patterned.

Pullman—passenger car owned and operated by the Pullman Company.

Pulse Power—a procedure in which a locomotive is given intermittent pulses of electric current.

Reefer—an insulated refrigerator car used for carrying perishable goods.

Remote Control Track—a section of track used for uncoupling and unloading cars.

Right of Way—precedence granted to one train to advance before another.

Rolling Stock—railway vehicles including passenger and freight cars.

Round House—engine shed where locomotives are stored when not in use.

Scale—the ratio in size between a model and a prototype.

Semaphore—railway signal with a pivoted arm that can be raised or lowered to warn an oncoming train.

Siding—section of track used for the temporary accommodation of trains.

Signal—means of controlling the movement of trains by warning or advising the engineer of the conditions ahead.

Stock Car—freight car used for the transporting of cattle and livestock.

Tank Car—freight car used for carrying liquids or gases in a tank-like container.

Tender—car that carries a freight locomotive's fuel and water supplies.

Terminal—the end of a railway line.

Throttle—a device that controls the speed of model train locomotives.

Tinplate—a term from the early days of model train production; used today to describe ready-to-run trains.

Transformer—a device for reducing standard household current.

Trestle—a wooden bridge over which trains ride.

The Nickel Plate Special™ train set, from Lionel trains, chugs along. Led by a black, die-cast steam locomotive with puffing smoke and an operating headlight, this engine is followed by a tender with steam sound effects, a yellow boxcar, a black gondola with canisters, a gray hopper and a red caboose. Featured in this set are trackside accessories and an operating crossing gate.

Truck—the assembly that supports a railway car and houses the wheels and axles.

Turnout—a section of track that switches out from the main line.

Turntable—a rotating device for turning locomotives around and placing them in a roundhouse.

Voltage—force that moves an electric current; measured in volts.

Yard—a group of tracks used for switching and storing railroad cars.

The Lionel Large Scale™ New York Central searchlight car features a powerful beacon that rotates 360 degrees and can be removed from the car and placed up to 5 feet from the track.

The Pennsylvania auto carrier from Lionel features a two-tiered auto carrier with 6 die-cast metal cars on board. The Tuscan-red carrier also has metal wheels and operating knuckle couplers.

The caboose is usually the last car of a freight train. This colorful Logo Caboose is one of the many fine freight cars offered by LGB.

An authentic Burger King model from Tyco. This contemporary building kit is available in HO gauge.

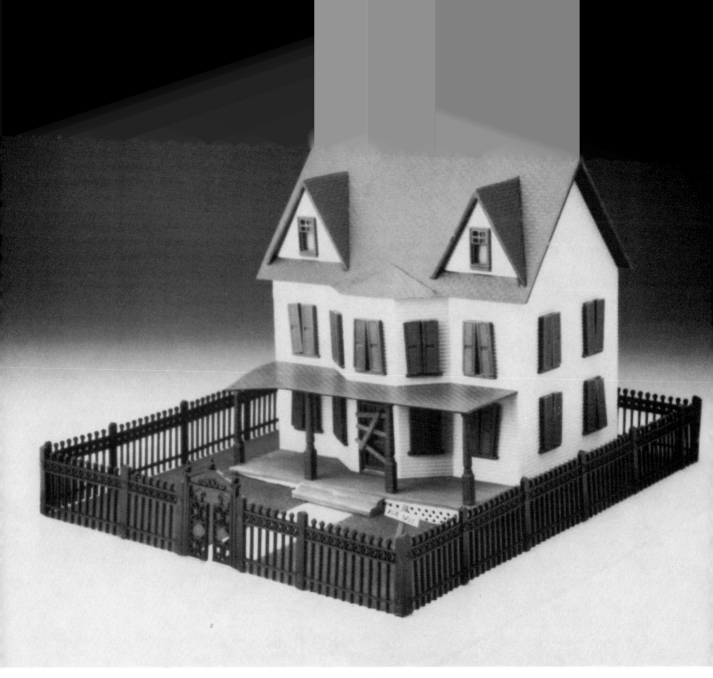

This Haunted House in HO scale from Model Power has everything but ghosts which you can add yourself for the last word in unusual enhancements.

Index